D0470622

Social Studies Activities
Kids Can't Resist!

by **Dee Benscoter and Geri Harris**

SCHOLASTIC
PROFESSIONAL BOOKS

NEW YORK   TORONTO   LONDON   AUCKLAND   SYDNEY
MEXICO CITY   NEW DELHI   HONG KONG   BUENOS AIRES

Acknowledgment

We would like to thank the students in our classes and Mrs. Gilbertson's class for trying our new activities and making samples for us to use.

We would also like to thank Gary and Ken for always supporting us in these endeavors, Ed and Nancy Olson for computer help, and all the teachers who willingly shared their expertise as we perfected this book.

Scholastic Inc. grants teachers permission to photocopy the designated reproducible pages from this book for classroom use. No other part of this publication may be reproduced in whole or in part, or stored in a retrieval system, or transmitted in any form or by any means, electronic, mechanical, photocopying, recording, or otherwise, without written permission of the publisher. For information regarding permission, write to Scholastic Inc., 557 Broadway, New York, NY 10012.

Cover design by Josué Castilleja
Interior design by Josué Castilleja
Interior illustrations by Tersea Southwell (page 59), Mike Moran (pages 19 and 32)
Map by Mapquest.com

ISBN 0-439-29703-6

Copyright © 2002 by Dee Benscoter and Geri Harris.
All rights reserved. Printed in the U.S.A.

2 3 4 5 6 7 8 9 10   40   09 08 07 06 05 04 03

CONTENTS

Introduction

Social Studies encompass a wide variety of topics and skills. In a world that has become increasingly smaller, students need to develop an understanding of our world's history and be familiar with the places in our world community. By doing so, they will be better enabled to make good decisions in the future.

One objective of this book is to help strengthen students' present understanding of maps, enhance their understanding of why things happened in the past, and give them a better idea of how these events have affected our lives today. Another objective is to fine-tune students' research and analytical skills. This book provides students with activities that involve various learning styles and opportunities to use higher level thinking skills. In some activities students are asked to combine their artistic talents with research, while other activities require them to use their reading skills to compare, contrast, and formulate opinions about the people and events of the past. By using evaluating skills, students will also develop an appreciation of history's notable personalities and their points of view. Throughout this book we have tried to touch on the following National Council of Social Studies strands:

- Culture
- Time, continuity, and change
- People, places, and environment
- Individual development and identity
- Power, authority, and governance
- Production, distribution, and consumption
- Global connections

The intent of this book is to integrate the knowledge and skills students have acquired in the classroom with their past experiences. It is our sincerest hope that this book will help students organize their thinking and develop the competencies they will need as citizens in an ever changing and interdependent world—and, hopefully, have fun in the process!

ABC Stories

A is for apple, **B** is for bear, **C** is for cat. Sounds familiar, right? But this is an ABC activity with a different twist. Students write the story of a historical event in exactly 26 sentences. The first sentence in the story starts with the letter **A**, the second sentence with the letter **B**, and so on through the letter **Z**. (The letter **X** may be too challenging, so you might accept a word that contains it.) Share with your students the example below.

Materials

- 8 $\frac{1}{2}$" x 11" loose-leaf notebook paper
- Pencil

Example

A long time ago, a man named Christopher Columbus had an idea that he could reach Asia by sailing west.

Being the educated man he was, he knew the world was round and not flat.

Carefully, he calculated how long the voyage would take.

During this time, he realized he would need assistance and financial support.

Each monarch he approached with his idea turned him down.

Finally, King Ferdinand and Queen Isabella of Spain agreed to provide him with ships.

Grateful for their help, Columbus promised to return with great riches.

He also said he would take the Catholic religion to the people in Asia.

In 1492, on August 3, Columbus started his trip.

Joining him were 89 sailors on 3 ships, the *Niña, Pinta,* and *Santa Maria.*

Keeping a journal, Columbus recorded the events of his voyage.

Long was the voyage, and his crew started to complain.

Mutiny was in the air.

Nearly two months at sea and no land was in sight but then . . .

On October 11, land was sighted.

Prayers of thanks were said for their safe trip.

Queen Isabella and King Ferdinand would surely reward Columbus for his discovery.

Realizing the importance of making friends with the people on the island, he gave them presents of glass beads and hawk's bells.

Since Columbus was convinced he had reached the Indies, he called the people Indians.

The next order of business was to get the Indians to lead him to the wealth of the Indies.

Until early 1493, Columbus explored the surrounding islands and . . .

Visited with the Indians that inhabited them.

When he returned to Spain, he demanded that he be named Admiral of the Sea.

X Exactly three more voyages were made by Columbus to the West Indies.

Years later, Amerigo Vespucci concluded that Columbus had not reached Asia but instead had discovered another continent.

Zeroing in on this conclusion, a German cartographer named the new continent America.

And the Answer Is . . .

Students always have fun when it comes to solving puzzles. In this activity, students write clues about the topics they have been studying in social studies and put them together in a puzzle for their classmates to solve.

1. Ask students to choose a person or place from a recent social studies unit.

   Example: The unit is Spanish explorers and the person is Cortés.

2. Next, have them record words that correspond to the unit. It is important to instruct students to choose words that contain a letter also found in the name of the person or place.

   Example: Aztecs, gold, China, Pizarro, silk, Mexico, and conquistador.

3. Then have students write clues (in question form) that correspond with the words.

   Example: Aztecs. Which Indians lived in Tenochtitlán?
   Gold. What precious metal were all Spanish explorers searching for?
   Silk. What cloth did Europeans want from Asia?
   China. Which country were Spanish explorers trying to reach by sailing west?
   Pizarro. Which explorer conquered the Incas?

4. Direct students to place a 1 under one of the letters in the answers that is the first letter in the person or place. Then have them place a 2 under a letter that is the second letter, a 3 under a letter that is the third letter, and so on.

5. Now have students rewrite their puzzle with the clues and numbers, and instruct them to leave out the answers.

Materials

- $8\frac{1}{2}$" x 11" loose-leaf notebook paper
- Pencil

Example

A z t e c s   Which Indians lived in Tenochtitlán?
    4 5

g o l d   What precious metal were all Spanish explorers searching for?
  2

s i l k   What cloth did Europeans want from Asia?
6

C h i n a   Which country were the Spanish explorers trying to reach by sailing west?
1

P i z a r r o   Which explorer conquered the Incas?
     3

The answer is C o r t é s
           1 2 3 4 5 6

7. Finally, have students exchange puzzles with one another and solve them.

SOCIAL STUDIES ACTIVITIES KIDS CAN'T RESIST! Scholastic Professional Books

Buddy Maps

Students love to design maps, and this activity gives them the chance to be creative and learn about geography.

1. Give each student a 12- by 9-inch sheet of paper.

2. Review cardinal directions with students.

3. Next, ask them to roughly draw in the geographical features on their map following your directions as you read the script written on the next page.

4. When you have completed the oral directions, have students use their rulers to make a map scale. They can determine how far it would be from one place to another.

5. Finally, have students write questions that another student will answer about the map.

Materials

- 12" x 9" white construction paper
- Ruler
- Pencil

Alternative Activities

• Use graph paper rather than plain paper. Ask students to put a letter grid going in one direction (from left to right), and a number grid running up and down. After they have drawn their objects on the paper, they should write questions that require another student to use the coordinates to find the object.

• Use seasonal objects on the map, such as flowers, pumpkins, scarecrows, leaves, and snowmen.

• Give students a list of features they need to place on the map, but allow them to decide where they will be placed.

Buddy Map Script

Read the following directions out loud, and have students make a small shape for each landform. Suggest that students use a pencil to roughly draw in the various geographical features; later they can add color and detail to the map.

1. Place a cardinal direction on each side of the paper.
2. Put a strait in the upper left corner.
3. Draw a dune in the center of the paper.
4. Place a desert in the lower right corner.
5. Draw a peninsula in the upper right corner.
6. Add an island south of the peninsula.
7. Make a lake southwest of the dune.
8. Draw a valley north of the dune, but not across from the strait.
9. Make a forest about 2 centimeters east of the dune.
10. Place a canal northwest of the desert.
11. Draw a delta by the island.
12. Put a river southwest of the dune and north of the lake.
13. Name each landform and add some color to the pictures.
14. Decide on the scale for your map. For example: 2 centimeters = 100 miles.
15. On a separate piece of paper, write 12 to 15 questions to ask others regarding the map.

Example

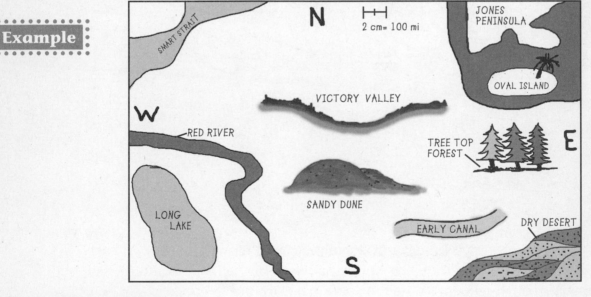

Sample Questions

- How far is it from the desert to the dune?
- If you traveled southwest from the peninsula, what geographical feature would you reach first?
- How many miles would you travel if you went from the river to the forest and then to the desert?
- Which direction would you travel to go from the island to the canal?

SOCIAL STUDIES ACTIVITIES KIDS CAN'T RESIST! Scholastic Professional Books

Career Moves

Imagine that a historical person has been given the opportunity to come into our modern world and live. Now he or she must find a job in today's market. What could he or she do?

1. Have students complete the Career Moves Job Application to discover the skills, training, and other valuable qualifications this person has.

2. Use the local newspaper's Help Wanted ads to find jobs that require those skills.

3. Direct students to write a paragraph explaining why this historical person would be qualified for this specific position. Students should be reminded that the person is seeking a career change.

Materials
- Career Moves Job Application
- Pencil
- Newspaper employment ads

Example

Name: Suzanne   Date: 2/16

Career Moves

Imagine that a historical person has been given the opportunity to come into our modern world and live. Now he or she must find a job in today's market. What could he or she do?

Job Application

Name: Abe Lincoln

Education: Home-schooled, self-taught lawyer

Skills: Builder of log homes, storyteller, mediator, politician, public speaker, writer, debater

Job-Related Experience: Farmer, store clerk, store owner, post master, surveyor, lawyer, politician

Military Experience: Captain in the Illinois volunteer militia. Commander in chief of military operations during the Civil War

Other Experience: _____

Possible Career Moves: Carpenter, construction worker, legal secretary, librarian, nanny

10

SOCIAL STUDIES ACTIVITIES KIDS CAN'T RESIST! Scholastic Professional Books

Alternative Activities

• Have students write a cover letter to go with their application. This letter should follow the business letter form. It would include the job the applicant is interested in, why the job interests the applicant, and a description of the specific skills the applicant has that are important for this job.

• Give students an opportunity to practice interview skills by asking them to role-play an interview of a historical person for a specific job.

Career Moves

Imagine that a historical person has been given the opportunity to come into our modern world and live. Now he or she must find a job in today's market. What could he or she do?

Job Application

Name: _____

Education: _____

_____

Skills: _____

_____

_____

Job-Related Experience: _____

_____

_____

Military Experience: _____

_____

Other Experience: _____

_____

Possible Career Moves: _____

_____

SOCIAL STUDIES ACTIVITIES KIDS CAN'T RESIST! Scholastic Professional Books

Changing History

What if your students were able to change the past? Which events would they change and what would the outcomes be? Pose these questions to your students, and then give them the opportunity to do just that. After studying a unit in social studies, have students brainstorm a list of events that took place. Next, encourage them to change the events so that the outcomes would have been much different. Have them explain how history might have been different as a result of these changes.

Materials
- 8½" x 11" loose-leaf notebook paper
- Pencil

······ **Sample Questions** ······

What if Abraham Lincoln had survived the gunshot wound he sustained from John Wilkes Booth?

CAUSE	HISTORICAL EFFECT
John Wilkes Booth's gun misfired.	1. Andrew Johnson never became president. 2. Lincoln would have been re-elected in 1864. 3. Reconstruction would have been easier on the South.

What if slavery had never been allowed in the United States?

CAUSE	HISTORICAL EFFECT
The Continental Congress disallowed slavery in the Declaration of Independence.	1. The Southern economy never flourished. 2. The Civil War never happened. 3. African-American men would have gotten to vote decades earlier.

What if our country had not doubled in size in 1803?

CAUSE	HISTORICAL EFFECT
France sold the Louisiana Purchase to Spain instead of the United States.	1. The United States would be half its size. 2. Mexico would be double its size. 3. Lewis and Clark never would have explored west of the Mississippi River.

Character Fact and Opinion

Characterizing a person requires using fact-and-opinion skills. In order to characterize someone, students need to analyze the person's actions and then form an opinion based on those actions. With this activity, students use their analytical skills to describe a historical figure.

Materials

— Character Fact and Opinion Worksheet

— Pencil

1. Give each student a copy of the Character Fact and Opinion worksheet.

2. Direct students to choose a historical figure from a unit previously studied.

3. Students should write the person's name in the blank circle at the center of the web.

4. Then, have students list actions of this person in the five circles going out from the center.

5. Instruct students to write words that describe this individual, based on each action, on lines drawn from the action bubbles.

Example

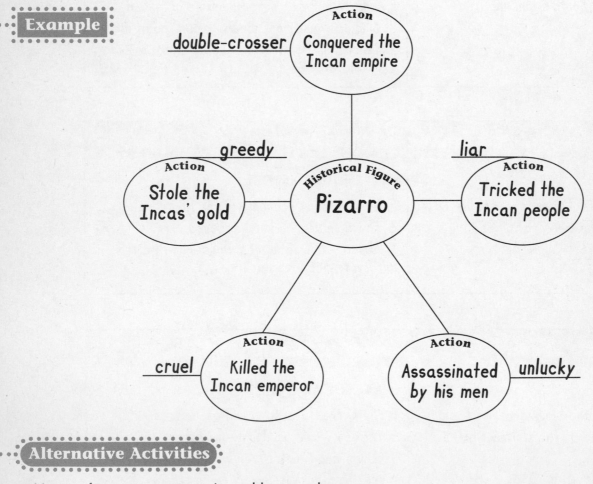

Alternative Activities

• Have a famous person reviewed by an adversary.

• Have a historical person look at a modern-day person.

Character Fact and Opinion

Choose a historical figure you have studied. Write the person's name in the center circle. In the five other circles, record five actions of this person. Then, connect words to each action bubble that describe this individual based on each action you recorded.

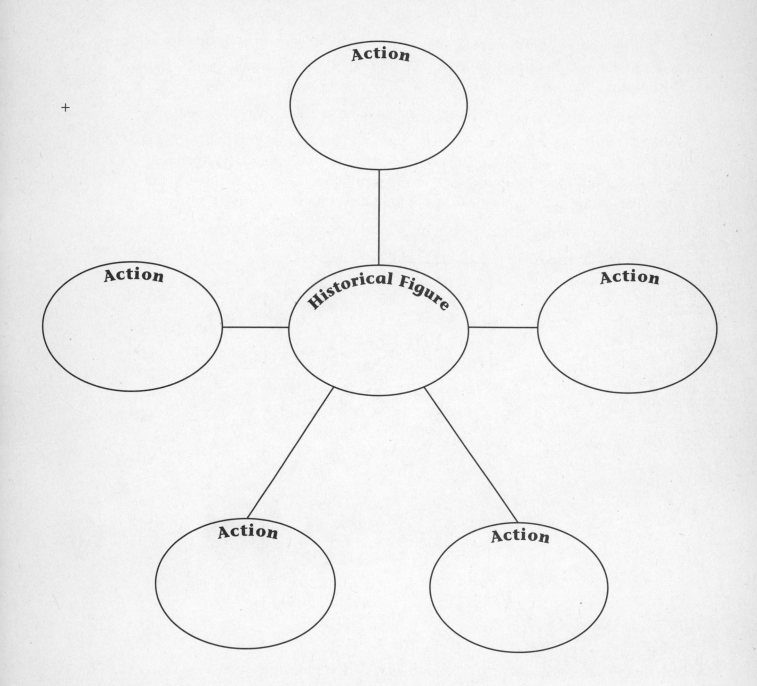

Culture Catalogs

Ask students if catalogs featuring a variety of goods have ever been delivered to their homes. Most of them will say yes. Ask students if they have ever seen a souvenir shop. Many students may have been to a souvenir shop while on vacation. This activity allows students to show their understanding of the culture they have been studying by creating a catalog of souvenir items that represent that culture.

Materials

– 9" x 12" white construction paper

– Colored pencils

1. First, ask students to brainstorm symbols, pictures, or slogans that might represent the people or culture they have studied, writing them on the board or on chart paper.

2. Next, have students brainstorm items that they have seen in souvenir stores.

3. Then, tell students they will each create a page in a class catalog that shows souvenir items representing people or groups they have studied. Have them draw pictures of souvenir items, such as mugs or pennants, and ask them to put slogans or symbols on the items that represent the cultures you have discussed.

4. Have them write a description about each product and include prices.

5. Bind their pages together in a class catalog.

Example

Spain

1. Cortes Cup $4.35
2. Conquerer Pillow $12.0
3. Stuffed Bull $15.30
4. Spanish Dancing Skirt $75.00

In the sixteenth century, many Spanish explorers traveled to the "new world" to claim fame + sometimes fortune.

5. Vespucci Telescope $30.99
6. Pizarro mini-billboard $15.00

Liz P.

Alternative Activities

• Have students design a catalog for a particular period in history such as Colonial America or Westward Movement.

• Give students a "budget" and let them "shop" from the class catalog. Ask them to explain why they chose each item.

Dictionary Fun

Few students enjoy being drilled on dictionary skills. In this activity, they can use those skills in a creative manner and won't realize they are practicing at the same time. First, students design a dictionary of people, places, and events from a particular time period and then draw conclusions to write opinion statements.

Materials

- 8 $\frac{1}{2}$" x 11" loose-leaf notebook paper
- Pencil
- 4 pieces of 8 $\frac{1}{2}$" x 11" white paper folded in half, stapled in the center

1. Discuss with students the information found in a dictionary, such as word pronunciation, parts of speech, definitions, and the use of words in context. Share with students the following example:

Example

> Marty H.
>
> Dictionary Fun
>
> 1. Re·vere, Paul (rē vere') (päwl) noun
>   1. a silversmith   2. a member of the Sons of Liberty   3. participant in the Boston Tea Party   4. warned colonists that the British were coming.
>
>   Paul Revere was the bravest patriot in the Revolutionary War.
>
> 2. La·fay·ette, Mar·quis, de (lah fā ĕt, mär kee, duh)
>   1. a French soldier   2. a French noble   3. volunteered to help Americans   4. George Washington's trusted advisor
>
>   During the Revolutionary War Marquis de Lafayette was America's best foreign friend.

2. Direct students to make a list of people, places, and events from a time period they have recently studied in social studies.

3. Next, have them arrange the items on the list in alphabetical order.

4. Then, tell students to write the first word (or words) followed by the pronunciation, part of speech, and three to four facts about the topic.

5. Have students write an opinion sentence about the topic using the facts from their definitions.

6. Encourage students to include the city, country, or colony where this topic would be found and to draw a picture of the person, place, or event.

7. Direct students to write similar entries for the other items on their list.

8. Give students paper that is bound together in booklet form in which to make their final copies. Remind students to put their entries in alpabetical order.

Fact and Opinion Switch

Students have a difficult time distinguishing between fact and opinion. In this activity, they make lists of facts and opinions for various topics and learn how to recognize the difference between them.

1. Share with students a story from the newspaper that lists specific facts, as well as a short editorial on the same subject.

2. Have students brainstorm how these two articles are different.

3. Remind students that facts are statements about something that can be proven, and opinions express how people feel or think about something.

4. Write a list of words that you might expect to see in an opinion article. This list might include such words as *favorite, best, hate, like, brave, worst,* and *mean.*

5. Divide students into two groups. Direct each of the students in one group to make a list of ten facts about the topic that you are studying.

6. Ask the other students to each write ten opinions about the topic.

7. Have the groups switch papers and change the opinions into facts and the facts into opinions.

Materials
- 8 $\frac{1}{2}$" x 11" loose-leaf notebook paper
- Pencil
- Newspaper articles, editorials, and news events

Example

Facts	Opinions
• George Washington was the leader of the Continental Army.	• George Washington was the best general in the Continental Army.
• Benedict Arnold first fought with the Americans but later joined the British.	• Benedict Arnold was a horrible man to become a traitor and join the British.
• Nathan Hale said, "I only regret that I have but one life to lose for my country."	• Nathan Hale bravely volunteered to spy on the British.

Flying High

Organizations and nations create flags to convey important information about themselves. Flags have symbols that represent the beliefs of the people, cultural information, and political views. These symbols can express the qualities that the people value. In this activity, students create several flags that represent their current social studies topic.

Materials
- 8 ½ " x 11" loose-leaf notebook paper
- Pencil
- Flying High Worksheet

1. Copy the Flying High worksheet for each student.

2. Show students a selection of flags from around the world or from the United States.

3. Discuss the patterns and symbols that are used on the flags. Note that most flags have only two or three colors and one or two symbols. Point out that some also have a motto or picture.

4. Create a list of possible symbols that would be appropriate for your current social studies theme.

5. List some people, events, or places that could have their own flags.

6. Have students create four flags that reflect something about the people, places, or events that they've been studying.

7. Underneath each flag, students should explain why they chose the colors, symbols, or motto that they did for each flag.

8. Display the flags on the wall for everyone to enjoy.

Example

Franklin Delano Roosevelt

The initials FDR represent his name. The stars in the corner remind us that he spent his life serving his country. A lightening bolt emphasizes his powerful leadership.

Flying High

Organizations and nations create flags to convey important information about themselves. Flags have symbols that represent the beliefs of the people, cultural information, and political views. These symbols can express the qualities that the people value. Create four flags that reflect something about the people, places, or events you've been studying. Describe the symbols used on each flag.

Fortunately/Unfortunately

There are always two sides to every story, and with every action there is a reaction. Sometimes the events seem to have good outcomes, but history shows this is not always so. In order to help them better appreciate history, encourage students to look at both sides of an issue. With this critical thinking activity, they need to analyze all of the outcomes and look at both sides of a historical event.

1. Read to students *Fortunately* by Remy Charlip.

2. Ask students to name a historical event with a successful outcome.

3. Have students list some unfortunate consequences that happened as a result of this event and discuss them as a class.

4. Direct students to choose several historical events from the unit they have been studying and write their own Fortunately/Unfortunately consequence books.

Materials

— *Fortunately* by Remy Charlip

— $8\frac{1}{2}$ " x 11" loose-leaf notebook paper

— Pencil

Example

Fortunately, the Union was preserved under Abraham Lincoln's leadership.

Unfortunately, Lincoln was shot five days after Lee surrendered.

Fortunately, his successor, Andrew Johnson, called for the Southern states to ratify the Thirteenth Amendment banning slavery in the nation.

Unfortunately, many Southern states passed "black codes," which limited the rights of the freed slaves.

Alternative Activities

• Try playing a "Fortunately/Unfortunately" game. First, divide the room into two sections. Put slips of paper with *fortunately* or *unfortunately* written on them in a basket. Each side will take a turn choosing a slip from the basket. The side that chooses "Fortunately" will come up with as many positive aspects as they can about a topic. The other side will come up with the negative aspects. Put a topic on the board and give students three minutes to brainstorm. The side with the most reasons gets a point for each reason.

• Have students work in groups to create a poster that shows the positive and negative sides to their topic.

Graffiti Wall

Would your students like to write on the walls? Would your students enjoy the opportunity to speak their minds? If the answer to both of these questions is yes, then they will enjoy this activity.

Materials

— Graffiti Wall Brick Template

— Colored pencils

1. Give each student a copy of the reproducible Graffiti Wall brick.

2. Assign—or allow students to choose—a famous person or an ordinary person from the time period they have been studying.

3. Have students think about issues that would have been important to the person they've chosen. It might be beneficial to have students discuss issues that would have been on the minds of people from that time period.

4. Ask students to decide on a statement, phrase, slogan, or symbol that the person they've chosen might have written on a public wall if given the opportunity to do so. Remind them that the purpose of *this* graffiti is to allow their chosen person to express personal opinions about issues that were important to him or her and to better understand the sentiments of people during that period of history. (It might be a good idea to emphasize that graffiti today is often considered vandalism. However, there are also condoned graffiti mural art projects throughout the country.)

5. Next, direct students to write their thoughts on their brick.

6. Last, attach the bricks in a staggered pattern on a wall to give the effect of a brick wall.

Example

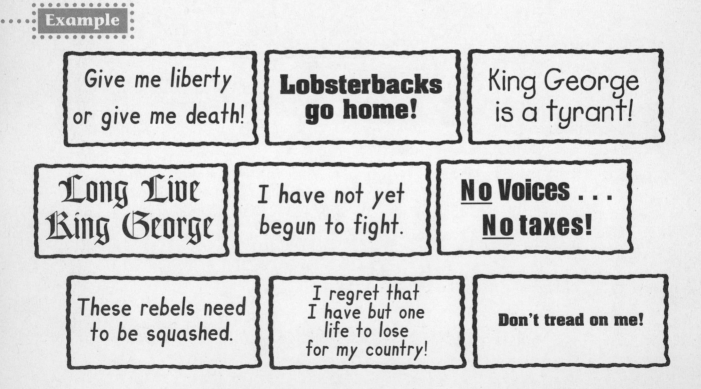

SOCIAL STUDIES ACTIVITIES KIDS CAN'T RESIST! Scholastic Professional Books

Name: _____

Date: _____

Graffiti Wall Brick

Think about some issues that might have been important to a person from a time period you have been studying. On the brick below, write a statement, phrase, slogan, or symbol that would express this person's point of view on an important issue.

Have You Heard? News Show

Students today are constantly hearing the news—broadcast through their TV, over the radio, and on the Web. In this activity, students create their own news show, then share their learning in a fun way.

Materials

8 ½" x 11" loose-leaf notebook paper

Pencil

1. Have students select important information from a topic they are covering in social studies. This could be a historical time frame, current events, or a specific place in the world.

2. From the list generated by the class, decide on three to five topics that would be newsworthy.

3. Then, ask students to work in pairs or small groups to create a news article. Each piece might include

- Pictures of people, events, or places
- Graphs showing the effects of each student's research
- A "live on the spot" report
- A display or real article from this newsworthy topic

4. Students can write the news stories together and decide how they should be broadcast. When everyone is ready, the show can be either taped or presented. The news show might have the following types of stories:

- A feature story
- A sports report
- A weather report
- Issues that relate to the topic
- Highlights of important events

Example

King Ferdinand's Nightly News Show

Stay tuned for the following stories:
1. Columbus is given three ships for a voyage to China and India.
2. Queen Isabella sells her jewels.
3. Sailors are needed for a ship sailing west.
4. What should we expect from the weather in Spain during September?
5. Rope-climbing contest is won by sailors of Madrid.
6. Spices are making dinners exciting in new restaurant in capital city.

Historical Diaries

For this activity, students take on the identity of a historical character while writing diary entries.

1. Ask students to choose a historical figure from a time period they have recently studied.

2. Direct them to write several diary entries for that person; have them include actual historical data from the character's life.

3. Explain to students that the diary entries should also express the character's thoughts, feelings, and secrets.

Materials

- 8 ½" x 11" loose-leaf notebook paper
- Pencil

Example

July 3, 1776

Dear Diary,
Tomorrow is the long-awaited day. After much debate and discussion, and, I might add, many heated arguments, the members of the Continental Congress will be voting on whether or not to ratify the document Ben Franklin, John Adams, Roger Sherman, and I have labored over—declaring the colonies' freedom from England. In my heart I know we are doing the right thing, but I would be fooling myself if I did not worry what the consequences of this action will be. I am also troubled about the removal of the slavery issue from this declaration. Will we live to regret this decision?

As always,
Thomas Jefferson

December 24, 1776

Dear Diary,
My heart is very heavy. Tomorrow I will be leading my men across the freezing waters of the Delaware River to attack the Hessians encamped in New Jersey. I worry because my men's clothes are ragged, and many have boots that are so worn they can hardly offer any protection from the elements. They are tired and many are ill. Will they be able to muster the strength needed for this mission? I am counting on the Hessians not anticipating our approach, hoping they will be sleeping off their celebration of Christmas. With a little luck, we will be able to carry out this attack with few American casualties.

Sincerely,
George Washington

Historical Theme Park

Today's students are always excited about taking trips to famous theme parks. In this activity, students use their knowledge of a historical event to create a theme park based on that event. The theme park will present, in chronological order, the places, people, and events that took place during that time frame.

1. Have students brainstorm a list of the most important people, places, and events that took place during the historical era you have been studying.

2. Next, have students write two or three sentences that sum up the key points from the list they've created.

3. Have students draw their theme park on a 12- by 18-inch sheet of construction paper.

4. Remind them to include the types of features that theme parks might have, such as pathways, rides, park areas, shops, video arcades, and museums.

5. Tell them to name each point of interest throughout the park based on one of the events previously selected, and to write descriptive sentences next to it.

6. Be sure to have students put all of the events on the map in chronological order, as on a time line.

7. Have students add a map legend or key to help tourists as they walk through their historical theme park.

Materials

- 9" x 12" or 12" x 18" white construction paper
- Colored pencils

Example

The American Revolutionary Theme Park

LEXINGTON FERRIS WHEEL

SECOND CONTINENTAL CONGRESS ROLLER COASTER

On May 10, 1975, the Second Continental Congress sent a petition to King George explaining America's grievances.

PAUL REVERE CAROUSEL

On April 18, 1775, Paul Revere, William Dawes, and Dr. Samuel Prescott spread the warning that the British were heading toward Concord.

On April 19, 1775, British troops met 70 minutemen on Lexington Green.

FORT TICONDEROGA SHOPS

On May 10, 1775, Benedict Arnold, Ethan Allen, and others captured Fort Ticonderoga without firing a shot.

Hourglass Biography Poems and Dolls

Many of us dream about what it might be like to live in a different time in history. In this project, students have an opportunity to write a poem about someone who might have lived in the past. After they complete the poem, students can create a paper doll that represents the person in their biography poem.

Poem

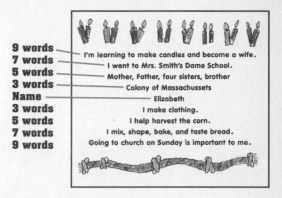

9 words	I'm learning to make candles and become a wife.
7 words	I went to Mrs. Smith's Dame School.
5 words	Mother, Father, four sisters, brother
3 words	Colony of Massachussets
Name	Elizabeth
3 words	I make clothing.
5 words	I help harvest the corn.
7 words	I mix, shape, bake, and taste bread.
9 words	Going to church on Sunday is important to me.

- Have students research information for a specific time in history.

- Next, students can "create" a person who might have lived during that period. They should include such things as the individual's job or career, responsibilities the person had, where the person lived, and some historical events that took place during that time frame.

- Ask students to write the information about their person in the hourglass form.

- Students may place their information in any order on the hourglass, except that the name of the person should be in the middle portion.

Biography Doll

- Ask students to trace the paper doll pattern (page 26) on a piece of card stock or posterboard and cut it out.

- Have students design a costume that would be appropriate for this time in history. Students need to consider the character's place in society and the information they have stated in the biography when they make the costume.

- Have students create the costume with cloth or construction paper and add other items such as hair or props that might have been used by the person. Suggested items include felt, scraps of material, yarn for hair, miniature equipment such as shovels, hammers, or baskets, and colored pencils to be used for the facial features.

Materials

- Doll pattern
- Scraps of cloth, yarn, felt, construction paper
- Colored pencils

Biography Doll Pattern

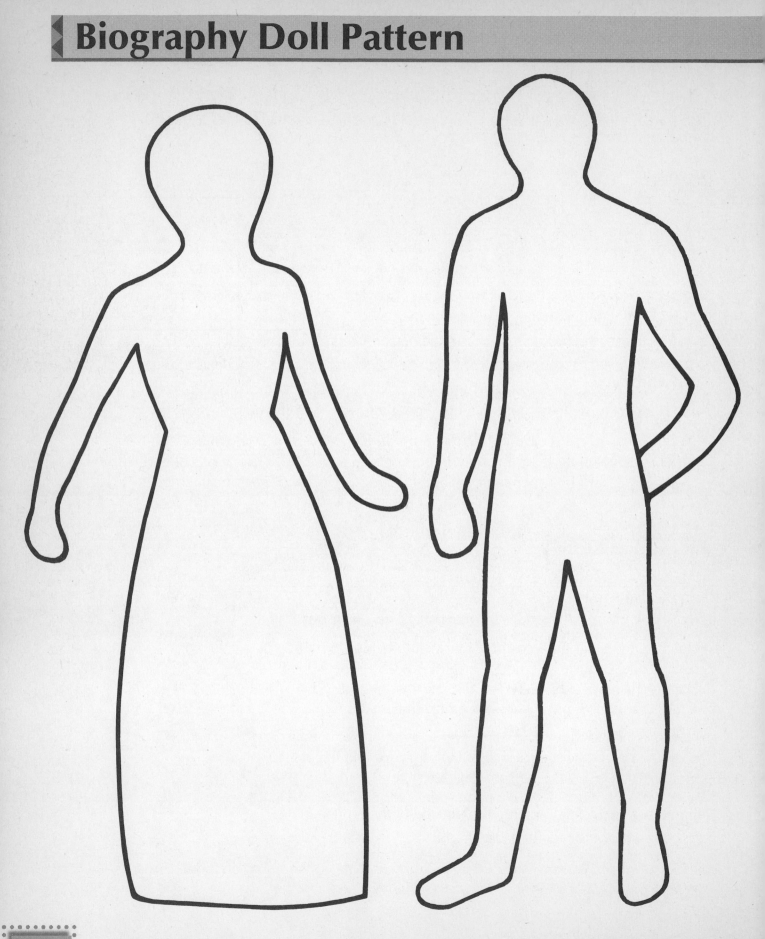

"I Won!"

Everyone gets excited about contests and the opportunity to win something. In this activity, each student wins an imaginary $10,000 trip for two. They will use the information learned in their social studies lessons, as well as research and math skills, to plan the cost of the trip.

1. Bring in some travel brochures for various parts of the United States.

2. Tell students to imagine that they have just won a $10,000 trip for two to anywhere in the United States and their objective is to make an itinerary for the trip using all of the money.

3. Have students look through brochures and decide where they'd like to go.

4. Give each student a copy of the U.S. world map worksheet (see page 63) and have them chart their itinerary on the map.

5. Give students the opportunity to research travel costs on the Web or from local travel agencies. Some brochures will have that information for the students to use.

6. Give each student an expense sheet so he or she can record what the cost of visiting each place would be.

7. Ask each student to make a presentation to the class about the trip and the destination. They should include the order in which they'll visit each place, tell what they want to do while there, and discuss the expense sheet for the trip.

Materials

- Travel brochures
- "I Won!" Expense Sheet
- U.S. Outline Map
- Pencil
- Atlas and information books

Example

Name:	Nolan		Date:	May 1

"I Won!" Expense Sheet

Destination __Lake Tahoe__   Length of Stay __2 days__

Expenses:
Travel
Lodging per day __$150.00__ x length of stay = __$300.00__

Meals
Breakfast	$7.00
Lunch	$8.00
Dinner	$20.00
Total	$35.00

Meals per day __$35.00__ x length of stay = __$70.00__

Entertainment activity __Tram__ Cost __$12.00__

Entertainment activity __Vikingsholm__ Cost __$3.00__

Total __$385.00__

Alternative Activities

- Encourage students to plan a trip outside of the United States.

- Select specific regions of the United States or world for the trip.

- Have students plan to send a postcard (they can create their own on index cards) of one natural resource or product from each place they visit.

Name: _____ Date: _____

"I Won!" Expense Sheet

Destination _____ Length of Stay _____

Expenses:
Travel
Lodging per day_____ x length of stay = _____
Meals

      Breakfast _____

      Lunch   _____

      Dinner   _____

      Total   _____

Meals per day_____ x length of stay = _____
Entertainment activity _____ Cost _____
Entertainment activity _____ Cost _____

                                   Total _____

Name: _____ Date: _____

"I Won!" Expense Sheet

Destination _____ Length of Stay _____

Expenses:
Travel
Lodging per day_____ x length of stay = _____
Meals

      Breakfast _____

      Lunch   _____

      Dinner   _____

      Total   _____

Meals per day_____ x length of stay = _____
Entertainment activity _____ Cost _____
Entertainment activity _____ Cost _____

                                   Total _____

SOCIAL STUDIES ACTIVITIES KIDS CAN'T RESIST! Scholastic Professional Books

In My Defense

There are two sides to every story. This holds true even in history. Unfortunately, the antagonist usually does not get to tell his side of the story or his reasons for behaving as he did. For this activity, students look at an event from the "bad guy's" point of view and write justifications for his actions.

Materials
- 8½" x 11" loose-leaf notebook paper
- Pencil

1. Lead a class discussion about point of view and have students discuss how events are usually viewed differently by different people. Remind students that people usually behave according to their beliefs.

2. Have students make lists of people that are considered "bad guys" from the historical period they have been studying.

3. Ask them to choose one person from their list and think about what this person's point of view might have been.

4. Have students write several statements from this person's point of view justifying his or her actions in history.

The Conquering of the Aztecs by Hernan Cortés

I have no idea why historians have portrayed me as a villain. Let's look at the facts. The Aztecs had no appreciation or need for all that gold. They had more than they could ever use. They did not realize what they had. Why should all that wealth be wasted? These people were the barbarians, not me. They killed their own people for the sake of their heathen gods. How can I be called a murderer when the Aztecs killed one another for no good reason? Despite the fact I brought along priests willing to help the Aztecs, they often rejected my help. They are so misguided that at one point they thought I was a god! Can you believe that? These people are very ignorant.

Alternative Activities

- Divide students into groups and have them write a play that is a trial about a historical "bad guy." Remind students to include witnesses that present different points of view.

- Divide the class into two debate groups. Assign one the task to debate in the defense of a notorious historical figure. Assign the opposite task to the other group, having them criticize the character and actions of the same person.

Letters From the Past

Students love to talk and write notes, so why not give them the chance to chatter while demonstrating their knowledge of the historical material they have studied?

1. Group students in pairs.

2. Ask them to choose two characters from the time period they are currently studying, with each of them taking on one of the identities.

3. Have each student write a letter to the other historical person. (One letter initiates the correspondence, the other letter responds to the first.) Direct students to include three facts that correspond with this pair's historical event.

4. When completed, have students share their letters with the class.

Materials

- 8 ½ " x 11" loose-leaf notebook paper
- Pencil
- Stationery

Example

October 13, 1492

Dear Queen Isabella,

It is with a joyous heart that I am writing to you today. After many difficult weeks crossing the great Atlantic Ocean, I have finally reached the Indies. My men and I were greeted by savages, who were scantily dressed. They were very excited to see us and have been very gracious hosts. I plan to get these Indians to lead me to the riches of the great Khan, and it won't be long before I will bring these treasures back to you.

Your faithful servant,
Christopher Columbus

December 22, 1492

Dear Christopher,

King Ferdinand and I were delighted when we heard of your discovery. I knew that you would not let me down when I sold my jewels for you. As you know, King Ferdinand was very skeptical about financing your voyage. With your success in reaching Asia, he can no longer have doubts about you. I am glad that the three ships we provided proved to be seaworthy. I have great plans for a huge celebration upon your return to Spain. Godspeed, dear Christopher.

Your Queen,
Isabella

Menu Trivia

Students can learn from everyday activities. For example, when visiting an ethnic restaurant, one often learns about the culture from trivia printed on the menu or place mat. In this activity, students display their knowledge of a country's agricultural products by creating a menu for the nation they are studying and by including trivia about the nation as part of the menu design.

Materials

— 9" x 12" white construction paper

— Colored pencils

— Almanac

1. Direct students to investigate the agricultural products that are produced in a country or region they have studied. (An almanac will be helpful for this activity.)

2. Have students create dishes that include one or more of the products produced in this region.

3. Instruct students to fold a 9- by 12-inch sheet of white construction paper in half, then design an attractive menu cover.

4. On the inside and back cover of the menu, students should list the names of the dishes that are available, major ingredients that are used in the dishes, and the cost.

5. In addition to the various dishes, trivia regarding the region should be written for the customer's enlightenment.

Example

Welcome to . . . .

Yubec's

The best restaurant in town!

Our Dessert Menu . . . . .

Desserts

Yellowhammer Cake $3.89
Yellowhammer is Alabama's nickname.

Anchorage Brownie $2.50
Anchorage is Alaska's largest city.

Houston Ice Cream $3.00
Houston is Texas' largest city.

Mount Elbert Pie $5.65
Mount Elbert is Colorado's highest point.

Beehive Cream Pie $4.25
Beehive State is Utah's nickname.

Charlotte's Chocolate Crunch Cookie $2.50
Charlotte is North Carolina's largest city.

Mirror, Mirror

In the fairy tale *Snow White*, the evil stepmother depended on her mirror for positive reinforcement and advice. A fun way to reinforce what students have learned is to have them give advice or offer suggestions to historical figures who come to them with their problems.

1. Duplicate one or two copies of the Mirror, Mirror worksheet for each student.

2. Prior to this activity, collect some advice columns from newspapers or magazines.

3. Share with your students some letters from the advice columns, highlighting both the questions and the answers.

4. Have students brainstorm a list of people from history who have encountered problems.

5. Discuss the problems and how these people might have felt.

6. Direct students to choose several people from the list or come up with their own ideas. Tell them to write conversations between these people and their "mirrors," with the historical figures stating their problems and the mirror giving advice.

7. After they have finished, ask students to draw the reflection of one of the figures they've chosen on the Mirror, Mirror Worksheet and then fill in the dialogue boxes.

8. Call upon students to share their projects with the class.

Materials

— Mirror, Mirror Worksheet

— Newspaper or magazine advice columns

— Colored pencils

Example

Mirror: Be persistent. Use the written word. Tell women to bombard the legislature with letters. Get your friends together, make signs and march.

Susan B. Anthony: The men just won't listen. Women deserve the right to vote. How do I convince them to pass a law for women to vote?

Alternative Activities

• Have each student write a conversation between two historical figures from two different time periods, one requesting advice and the other answering the plea.

• Ask students to write an advice column where people from the present write to a historical person who has the same occupation, asking for help with their present-day career problems.

News and Views

Most of us like to hear what's going on in Hollywood. We read gossip about movie stars in magazines and newspapers and watch it on TV. This activity allows students to use the knowledge they have gained from a topic in social studies and adapt it to a gossip format.

1. Make a copy of the News and Views worksheet for each student.

2. Prior to starting this activity, bring in some short gossip articles. These might include stories from movie magazines or from the lifestyle or arts section of the newspaper.

3. After you have shared some of the articles, have students discuss the types of things these articles include, such as who's dating whom, who's working where, who's accomplished what, or who's mad at whom.

4. Give students a list of people or events from their social studies lessons.

5. Have students create a bit of gossip that might be circulating about one of the people or events.

6. Ask students to put their gossip scoop in the newspaper column-style worksheet.

7. Suggest that they add a picture to make the gossip page more interesting.

Materials

– News and Views Worksheet
– Colored pencils
– Samples of newspaper front pages

Example

The Spanish Happenings — May, 1492

News and Views

Puzzle Geography

For a different assessment idea, have your students use their knowledge of a nation to create a puzzle.

1. Select the topics that you would like to have your students include in puzzles. These might include

- Agricultural products
- Capital city
- Climate
- Cultural facts
- Education
- Exports
- Famous people
- Flag
- Government
- Holidays
- Imports
- Monetary units
- Natural resources
- Physical geography
- Population
- Religion

2. Give students a 12- by 18-inch sheet of white construction paper.

3. Have students draw a puzzle of 10 to 16 large puzzle pieces on their paper.

4. Direct students to write the name of a different topic and a fact about the topic on each puzzle piece.

5. Tell students to create a drawing on each puzzle piece that represents the topic. For example, they could draw several people to represent population.

6. When the puzzle is finished, instruct them to cut apart each of the puzzle pieces.

7. Have students switch puzzles and try to assemble them.

Materials

- 12" x 18" white construction paper
- Colored pencils, crayons, or markers
- Scissors

Alternative Activities

Rather than making a puzzle about a specific nation, have students create a puzzle based on one of the following ideas:

- Continents
- Cultural activities
- Imports and exports from the continent
- Languages
- Physical geography, including rivers, mountains, oceans, and plateaus

Rebus Stories

Social studies is a subject filled with stories about people and events. Students love writing and telling stories. Why not combine the two for an activity that checks their comprehension of past events while giving them the opportunity to express themselves in a creative form? With this activity, students take their knowledge of a historical event and write a factual or historical fiction rebus story that uses pictures in place of some of the words.

Materials

— 8 ½" x 11" loose-leaf notebook paper

— Pencil

1. Explain to the class that rebus stories use pictures in place of some words.
2. Have students brainstorm events they have recently studied.
3. Ask them to each choose one event to write about in a short story.
4. Have each student make a list of the story elements and facts to include.
5. Direct students to write a rough draft of their stories.
6. After they have finished, tell students to go back and substitute simple pictures for 10 to 15 words in the story.
7. Finally, have students rewrite and share their final draft with the class.

Example

Alternative Activities

- Direct students to incorporate the vocabulary studied during this topic in their stories.
- Require students to include 8 to 10 landforms in the picture sections of their story.

Regional Trees

Your students know about apple trees, maple trees, and probably family trees, but have they ever created a regional tree? With this activity, students demonstrate their artistic abilities while applying the information they have learned about a particular region or country.

Materials

- 12" x 18" white construction paper

- Scraps of green, red, brown, yellow, or orange paper (for the leaves)

- 12" x 18" brown construction paper (for the trunk)

- Pencil

- Glue stick

1. Direct students to sketch and cut out a tree trunk and three main branches using brown construction paper.

2. Next, they should glue the trunk and branches onto a 12- by 18-inch sheet of white construction paper. The tree should fill most of the sheet.

3. Tell students to label one branch "Climate," one "Natural Resources," and the third branch "Physical Features."

4. Have them draw and cut out leaves large enough on which to write four or five words.

5. Instruct students to label each leaf with a fact about the region's climate, physical features, natural resources, or other suggested topic, and then glue them on the correct tree branch.

Other Topics

- Agricultural products
- Cultural facts
- Famous people
- Government
- Important historical events
- Manufacturing
- Religion

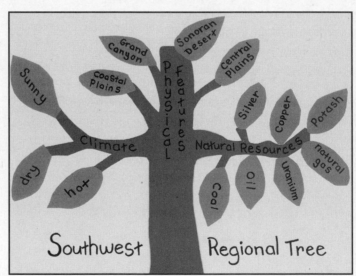

Alternative Activities

- Have students draw the leaves on the tree. If the region they are working on covers more than one country, state, or area, have students make a key for their project, and give each specific place a color.

- While studying American government, have students make branches of the government: Executive, Legislative, and Judicial. Direct students to write facts about each branch on the leaves and attach the leaves to the appropriate branches.

Shaped Time Line ▶

Creating a time line is an excellent way to check students' knowledge of a unit. In this activity, students create a time line with a twist.

Materials

- 12" x 18" white construction paper
- Colored pencils, crayons, or markers

1. Have students work together to come up with a list of people or events that took place in the era they have been studying. For example, they might list all the major explorers from 1000 AD to 1760 AD.

2. Tell students to put the events or people in order by date.

3. Explain to students that they can also use additional categories for sorting this data. For example, explorers could also be sorted according to their nationality or the nation for which they undertook their explorations.

4. Once students have organized the data, have them decide on a picture that will best represent their overall topic. For explorers, they might use a ship, or for the Civil War, they could use a flag or a cannon.

5. Have them draw the picture that represents their topic on a large piece of construction paper.

6. Then within the picture, students can draw the time line facts. For example, if the topic is explorers, the ship's hull can hold the time line.

7. Encourage your students to be creative and make their time lines a feast for the eyes as well as a product of knowledge.

Souvenir Shopping

Part of the fun of traveling to new places is shopping for souvenirs. Many souvenirs are manufactured from the region's natural resources; others represent places of interest or historical events. In this activity, your students travel to new places and buy representative souvenirs.

1. Choose a place of interest and ask students to find the latitude and longitude coordinates for each place. (You might want to ask students to list map coordinates as an alternative.)

2. Have students find the place on a natural resources map, and ask them to list products that can be found in this region.

3. Have them use various reference materials (encyclopedias or the Web) to find points of interest for this area or important historical events that happened there.

4. Finally, have them come up with a list of souvenir items that would represent this place.

5. Have students present their souvenirs to the class.

Materials

— Souvenir Shopping Worksheet
— Atlas
— Reference books
— Pencil

Example

Name: Joe L. Date: 4/30

Souvenir Shopping

Choose a continent, nation, or region. Pick ten places that you might visit in this area and locate their coordinates. As you list these places, organize them so that your trip is in a logical order. Use the product map in an atlas or a reference book to find this area's resources and the products it produces. You may also choose a point of interest or significant historical event that happened here. Then, choose an item that might be a souvenir representing this resource or historical event.

Tour   Southern United States

Place	Coordinates	Product/ Resource/ Event/Point of Interest	Souvenir
Crater of Diamonds, AR	34°N 93°W	diamonds	1 carat diamond
New Orleans, LA	29°N 90°W	jazz music	saxophone
Jackson, MS	32°N 90°W	cotton	cotton shirt
Huntsville, AL	34°N 86°W	U.S. Space Center	Shuttle model
Orlando, FL	28°N 81°W	oranges	orange juice
Atlanta, GA	33°N 84°W	peaches	peach pie
Savannah, GA	32°N 81°W	peanuts	jar of peanut butter
Charleston, SC	32°N 79°W	Sullivan Island	Revolutionary statue
Raleigh, NC	35°N 78°W	wooden furniture	rocking chair
Chincoteague, VA	37°N 75°W	wild horses	horse statue

41

SOCIAL STUDIES ACTIVITIES KIDS CAN'T RESIST! Scholastic Professional Books

Name: _____ Date: _____

Souvenir Shopping

Choose a continent, nation, or region. Pick ten places that you might visit in this area and locate their coordinates. As you list these places, organize them so that your trip is in a logical order. Use the product map in an atlas or a reference book to find this area's resources and the products it produces. You may also choose a point of interest or significant historical event that happened here. Then, choose an item that might be a souvenir representing this resource or historical event.

Tour _____

Place	Coordinates	Product/ Resource/ Event/Point of Interest	Souvenir
_____	_____	_____	_____
_____	_____	_____	_____
_____	_____	_____	_____
_____	_____	_____	_____
_____	_____	_____	_____
_____	_____	_____	_____
_____	_____	_____	_____
_____	_____	_____	_____
_____	_____	_____	_____
_____	_____	_____	_____

Then and Now

In this activity, students take an event or human activity from the past and compare it to a modern-day equivalent.

1. Select a topic within your current social studies lessons, such as government, race relationships, scientific concepts, or military changes.

2. Write a series of questions that address the way things were in the past and read them to the class.

3. Repeat the questions, this time addressing current ideas or philosophies.

4. Ask students to decide which attitudes or behaviors are still prevalent.

5. Finally, have students comment on how things could be improved or changed today.

Materials
- 8 $\frac{1}{2}$" x 11" loose-leaf notebook paper
- Pencil

Example

Our Government: Then (The House of Burgesses, circa 1600)	Our Government: Now
a. What freedoms did the people of the Virginia Colony want?	a. What freedoms do we want today?
b. Who could be a representative in the government?	b. Who can be a representative in the government?
c. How were representatives elected?	c. How are representatives elected?
d. What types of problems did they solve?	d. What types of problems do they solve?
e. Sum it all up in a few sentences.	e. Sum it all up in a few sentences.

Sample Questions

- What is the legacy from the House of Burgesses for our own government today?
- Share two things we have today that you think are an improvement over the House of Burgesses? Why are they an improvement?

SOCIAL STUDIES ACTIVITIES KIDS CAN'T RESIST! Scholastic Professional Books

There Must Be a Better Way

Not everything in life today happens as planned. The same is true in history. As long as humans have been on earth, they've made mistakes. By studying historical mistakes, we hope that future generations will not repeat these blunders. In this activity, students look at historical plans or events that went wrong and write alternative solutions for how the key players of the past could have avoided their problems. Then, students will evaluate the solutions and decide which one would have been the best. In other words, what could the people of the past have done differently to avert their problems?

Materials

- There Must Be a Better Way Worksheet
- Pencil

Example

Name: **Becky**   Date: **6/12**

There Must Be a Better Way

Think of a problem that people experienced in the period of history you have been studying. Write it below. Next, think of three possible solutions and write them below. Then, rate the effectiveness of each solution and add up the scores to see which would be the best solution.

Problem: _Incan empire conquered by Spaniards_

Solution: _Build a 15-foot wall around the empire_

3 = Highly effective   2 = Somewhat effective   1 = Not effective

Is it safe?	③	2	1
Is it cost-effective?	3	②	1
Is it quick?	3	2	①
Will it work?	③	2	1

TOTAL SCORE **9**

Solution: _Require all citizens to serve in the military_

3 = Highly effective   2 = Somewhat effective   1 = Not effective

Is it safe?	3	②	1
Is it cost-effective?	3	②	1
Is it quick?	3	②	1
Will it work?	3	②	1

TOTAL SCORE **8**

Solution: _Atahuallpa and Huascar unite and attack the Spaniards first_

3 = Highly effective   2 = Somewhat effective   1 = Not effective

Is it safe?	3	②	1
Is it cost-effective?	③	2	1
Is it quick?	3	②	1
Will it work?	③	2	1

TOTAL SCORE **10**

SOCIAL STUDIES ACTIVITIES KIDS CAN'T RESIST! Scholastic Professional Books

There Must Be a Better Way

Think of a problem that people experienced in the period of history you have been studying. Write it below. Next, think of three possible solutions and write them below. Then, rate the effectivness of each solution and add up the scores to see which would be the best solution.

Problem: _____

Solution: _____

3 = Highly effective	2 = Somewhat effective	1 = Not effective

Is it safe?   3   2   1

Is it cost-effective?   3   2   1

Is it quick?   3   2   1

Will it work?   3   2   1

TOTAL SCORE_____

Solution: _____

3 = Highly effective	2 = Somewhat effective	1 = Not effective

Is it safe?   3   2   1

Is it cost-effective?   3   2   1

Is it quick?   3   2   1

Will it work?   3   2   1

TOTAL SCORE_____

Solution: _____

3 = Highly effective	2 = Somewhat effective	1 = Not effective

Is it safe?   3   2   1

Is it cost-effective?   3   2   1

Is it quick?   3   2   1

Will it work?   3   2   1

TOTAL SCORE _____

SOCIAL STUDIES ACTIVITIES KIDS CAN'T RESIST! Scholastic Professional Books

A Ticket to Ride

Planning a vacation to an exotic place is always fun. In this activity, students reinforce their skills using latitude and longitude, and identify interesting things about a chosen destination.

1. Have students select six or more places from a continent, nation, or U.S. region.

2. Ask students to find the latitude and longitude lines for each place.

3. Have students use white paper cut into 3- by 5-inch rectangles to illustrate a point of interest, product, or natural resource from the area they've chosen.

4. On a piece of 9- by 12-inch colored construction paper, mount the drawings and have students write several sentences that tell why they'd like to visit the place, as well as several important facts.

Materials

– 3" x 5" white paper

– 9" x 12" colored construction paper

– Colored pencils

– Optional: a world map

Example

49 N 2 E

I would like to visit the Eiffel Tower in Paris, France. The tower was built for the 1889 International Exhibit in Paris. It commemorates the centenary of the French Revolution. It took two years to complete, and there are 1,652 steps to the top. I think Paris would be interesting because it is the capital of France. While there, I would also like to visit the river Seine, and see the artwork in the Louvre.

Top Ten Reasons

Students are often curious about why people from the past behaved as they did. To better understand history, students should look at historical figures' personalities, their ethics, and the events of the time period. With this activity, students analyze and evaluate the motives and behaviors of people who lived in earlier periods.

Materials
- 8 $\frac{1}{2}$" x 11" loose-leaf notebook paper
- Pencil

1. Begin by having the students brainstorm a list of events that occurred during a time period they have recently studied.

2. Discuss why people from this period might have behaved the way they did. Have students reflect on traits, beliefs of the period, and cause-and-effect relationships.

3. Share the example below with the class.

Top Ten Reasons Columbus Did Not Find Asia

10. Became destitute and could no longer explore
9. Felt pressure from Spain and fortune seekers to find treasures quickly
8. Lacked accurate information about the people and land of Asia
7. Didn't have reliable scientific equipment
6. Had no one with him that he trusted as an adviser
5. Too stubborn to seek advice from other explorers
4. Too proud to consider that he had made a mistake
3. Self-denial that he had not reached the Indies
2. Miscalculated the size of the earth
1. Unaware there were two continents between Europe and Asia going west

4. Divide students into groups of two or three.

5. Have students choose an event from the list or come up with one of their own, then direct them to create a list of ten reasons why this event might have happened. Encourage them to be innovative and critical as well as factual. (Ask students for five reasons if they have difficulty thinking of ten.)

6. After students have finished, tell them to order their list from 10 to 1. Each reason should be progressively more important with 1 being the main reason the event happened.

7. Have students share their lists with the class.

Top Hits Countdown

Combine a little music exploration with students' knowledge of social studies and you will have some truly hot hits. This activity gives students the opportunity to rename historical events by changing them into song titles.

1. Discuss with the class why a song has a particular title (for example, it could be a line from the song).

2. Have students brainstorm topics and events recently studied in social studies and list them on a chart or chalkboard.

3. Ask students to choose several items from the list.

4. Tell students to create song titles that would be appropriate to characterize their choices. You can share with students the examples below.

Materials

- 8$\frac{1}{2}$" x 11" loose-leaf notebook paper
- Pencil

Example

"I Want to Live Forever"—Ponce de Leon was searching for the fountain of youth in Florida, but unfortunately he never discovered the magical water.

"$\frac{2}{3}$ Is My Favorite Number"—A bill needs $\frac{2}{3}$ of the House of Representatives and $\frac{2}{3}$ of the Senate to vote yes before the President can sign the bill into a law.

"I'd Rather Be an Emperor"—Napoleon Bonaparte made himself emperor of France after he was originally named president.

"Look to the Sun"—The Egyptians worshipped Amon-Re, the sun god who was the main god of Egypt.

5. After each song title, have students write a brief description of the actual topic or event.

6. Ask students to share their titles with the class so that others can try to guess what the titles represent.

Alternative Activities

- Students can write lyrics to go with the song titles.

- Divide students into groups of three or four. Have them take the activity one more step by writing lyrics for two or three more stanzas.

Trivia Scavenger Hunt

With this activity, students race against the clock and their fellow classmates to answer as many trivia questions as they can. The biggest question of all is, "Who will win?"

1. First, decide if you want students to do research on the Web or work with a variety of reference and trade books. If you decide to have them use books, it works more smoothly to have the books gathered and available for students.

2. Duplicate one copy of the trivia questions for each pair of students.

3. Discuss with the class how a scavenger hunt works. (A team races against other teams to gather specified items. The team that gathers the most items within the specified amount of time wins.)

4. After dividing students into pairs, explain that they will be given a list of trivia questions and need to look for the answers in the reference books. Each team will receive one book. After five minutes, the teams will trade books and research in that book for five minutes. (The rotation of books should occur four times.)

5. Discuss with them the best ways to find the answers: through a book's index or its table of contents, or by skimming the material rather than reading the entire book. (If using the Web, bookmark appropriate sites ahead of time for students to access.)

6. Tell students to look over all the questions before beginning. Since students have limited access to each resource, suggest that they answer questions in the order they're found to make the best use of their time.

7. At the end of the period collect all papers. During the next class period, share the correct answers with the students as they check their answers.

Materials
- Trivia Scavenger Hunt Sheets
- Reference books
- Pencils

Answers

Name: Jerome   Date: 2/26
Trivia Scavenger Hunt: Martin Luther King, Jr.

Find as many answers as possible to the questions below. You have 20 minutes.

1. What name was Martin Luther King Jr. first given after he was born? **Micheal**
2. Martin's family had a nickname for him. What was it? **M.L.**
3. When Martin was born, his father was a Baptist minister. What job did his mother have? **school teacher**
4. Why didn't Martin graduate from high school? **high scores on college entrance exam**
5. How old was Martin when he entered Morehouse College? **15**
6. Name the church Martin first co-pastored with his father. **Ebenezer Baptist**
7. What was the name of his bride, whom he married in 1953? **Coretta Scott**
8. Martin authored several books. What was the name of his first book? **Stride Toward Freedom: The Montgomery Story**
9. While Martin was promoting this book in Harlem, an African-American woman stabbed him. What was her name? **Izola Ware Curry**
10. Martin mirrored his nonviolent action after what Indian political leader? **Ghandi**
11. How many times was Martin arrested for taking part in civil rights protests? **4**
12. In what year did he win the Nobel Peace Prize? **1964**
13. Martin delivered many famous speeches. His most famous was his "I Have a Dream" speech. Where did he deliver this speech? **Washington, DC**
14. Martin was assassinated on April 4, 1968. Who shot him? **James Earl Ray**
15. Martin was standing on the balcony of a motel in Memphis, Tennessee, when he was shot. What was the name of this motel? **Lorraine Motel**
16. Why was Martin in Memphis on the day that he was shot? **trash workers' strike**
17. In which city was Martin's assassin captured in June 1968? **London**

SOCIAL STUDIES ACTIVITIES KIDS CAN'T RESIST! Scholastic Professional Books   49

Name: Shanice   Date: 5/28
Trivia Scavenger Hunt: U.S. Regions

Find as many answers as possible to the questions below. You have 20 minutes.

1. How many states make up the northeast region of the United States? **9 states**
2. Which two regions combined have the most states? **The Southern and Western regions**
3. Which region is directly north of Mexico? **The West**
4. In which region would you find the Grand Canyon? **The West**
5. Mount McKinley is the tallest mountain in the United States. In which region will you find it? **The West**
6. The Red River is the border between which two states in the southwestern region? **Oklahoma and Texas**
7. The Black Hills are low mountains that got their name from the pine trees covering them, which make them look black. In which region are the Black Hills? **Mid-west**
8. New Orleans is the busiest seaport in the southeastern region. In which state will you find New Orleans? **Lousiana**
9. What is the nickname for the midwestern region? **The Heartland**
10. Which region has the lowest population? **Northeast**
11. In which region will you find the Great Lakes? **Mid-west**
12. The Sierra Nevada mountains run through which states? **California and Nevada**
13. Which state in the Pacific Northwest had volcanic activity in the last 20 years? **Washington**
14. Rhode Island is made up of how many square miles? **48 miles long and 37 miles long**
15. Which minerals and fossil fuels can be found in the southeastern region? **Natural gas, oils, salt, sulfur, lead zinc, bauxite and coal**

SOCIAL STUDIES ACTIVITIES KIDS CAN'T RESIST! Scholastic Professional Books   50

Name: _____ Date: _____

Trivia Scavenger Hunt: Martin Luther King, Jr.

Find as many answers as possible to the questions below. You have 20 minutes.

1. What name was Martin Luther King, Jr. first given after he was born? _____

2. Martin's family had a nickname for him. What was it?_____

3. When Martin was born, his father was a Baptist minister. What job did his mother have?

   _____

4. Why didn't Martin graduate from high school?_____

5. How old was Martin when he entered Morehouse College?_____

6. Name the church Martin first co-pastored with his father. _____

7. What was the name of his bride, whom he married in 1953?_____

8. Martin authored several books. What was the name of his first book?

   _____

9. While Martin was promoting this book in Harlem, an African-American woman stabbed
   him. What was her name?_____

10. Martin mirrored his nonviolent action after what Indian political leader?

    _____

11. How many times was Martin arrested for taking part in civil rights protests?_____

12. In what year did he win the Nobel Peace Prize? _____

13. Martin delivered many famous speeches. His most famous was his "I Have a Dream"
    speech. Where did he deliver this speech?_____

14. Martin was assassinated on April 4, 1968. Who shot him?_____

15. Martin was standing on the balcony of a motel in Memphis, Tennessee, when he
    was shot. What was the name of this motel?_____

16. Why was Martin in Memphis on the day that he was shot? _____

17. In which city was Martin's assassin captured in June l968? _____

Trivia Scavenger Hunt: U.S. Regions

Find as many answers as possible to the questions below. You have 20 minutes.

1. How many states make up the northeast region of the United States?_____

2. Which two regions combined have the most states?_____

3. Which region is directly north of Mexico?_____

4. In which region would you find the Grand Canyon?_____

5. Mount McKinley is the tallest mountain in the United States. In which region will you find it?

_____

6. The Red River is the border between which two states in the southwestern region?

_____

7. The Black Hills are low mountains that got their name from the pine trees covering them, which make them look black. In which region are the Black Hills?

_____

8. New Orleans is the busiest seaport in the southeastern region. In which state will you find New Orleans?_____

9. What is the nickname for the midwestern region?_____

10. Which region has the lowest population?_____

11. In which region will you find the Great Lakes? _____

12. The Sierra Nevada mountains run through which states?_____

13. Which state in the Pacific Northwest had volcanic activity in the last 20 years?

_____

14. Rhode Island is made up of how many square miles?_____

15. Which minerals and fossil fuels can be found in the southeastern region?

_____

SOCIAL STUDIES ACTIVITIES KIDS CAN'T RESIST! Scholastic Professional Books

True/False

What student wouldn't enjoy having the opportunity to create a test for the rest of the class? Here is a class-tested, fun way to review material or just reinforce information. In this activity, students themselves write statements for their classmates to respond to with *true* or *false*.

1. Ask students to write ten or more true or false statements about a topic they have recently studied and include an answer key.

2. Divide students into groups of three or four.

3. Have each student take a turn reading his or her statements to the other students in the group. They each should record whether they believe it is true or false.

4. Finally, have the reader share the correct answers, while others in the group check their papers.

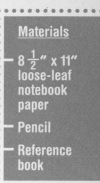

Materials

- 8 $\frac{1}{2}$″ x 11″ loose-leaf notebook paper
- Pencil
- Reference book

Example

Statement	True/False
1. The leader of the Cherokee nation was Chief John Ross.	True
2. Very few Indians died on the Trail of Tears journey in 1839.	False
3. The Cherokees were forced to move from Georgia to Oklahoma.	True

Alternative Activities

- Have each student share one or two statements with the entire class. After each student has read his or her own, correct the answers together.

- Have students write statements to try to stump the teacher, then read them aloud.

Web Pages

Many of today's young people are computer literate. This activity gives them a chance to consider what they have seen on the Web, and to design a Web page on paper.

1. Before beginning this activity, find some Web sites that you think are well done and some that are not.

2. Have students view these sites and, as a class, make a list of various elements on the sites. These might include

   - Main topic and home page
   - Pictures
   - Information regarding the topic
   - Added pages that the home page takes you to via icons
   - Various fonts and sizes of letters

3. Next, ask students to pick a topic for their Web site and then break their topic into subtopics. Those, in turn, can be broken into smaller topics.

4. Ask students to write a paragraph about each topic, as well as one for the main subtopics they want to cover on their Web site.

5. Give each student several pieces of construction paper and other art supplies to help create their Web pages.

6. Students should make "buttons" on the pages to show where they would send site visitors who want more information.

7. Students can use pictures from magazines for clip art or draw their own pictures.

Materials

- 9" x 12" colored or white construction paper
- Magazines
- Colored pencils
- Index cards

Example

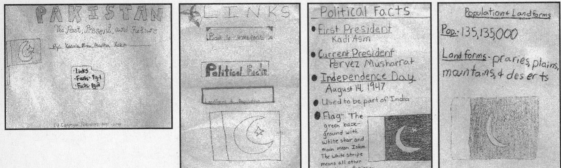

8. Display each complete Web page with an index card next to it. Then, have the class "visit" each site and write one comment saying what they like about it.

9. If you are able to set up a Web page, you can assign a group of students to do one particular part of the site and then put it on the Web for the school community and parents to enjoy.

What's Happening?

The newspaper is an important resource tool for students. In this activity, they can use the newspaper to find places around the world, and then apply their math skills to create a graph.

1. Give each student a copy of the newspaper.

2. Have each student make a list of the cities and nations that the news articles highlight.

3. Then, have them use a world map to find the continent on which each place is located.

4. Next, give each child a piece of graph paper.

5. Ask students to write the names of the continents across the bottom of the graph paper, and to number the graph lines by tens going up the sides.

6. Students should then graph the number of times each continent has appeared in the news.

Materials

— Newspapers
— World map or atlas
— Graph paper
— Colored pencils

Example

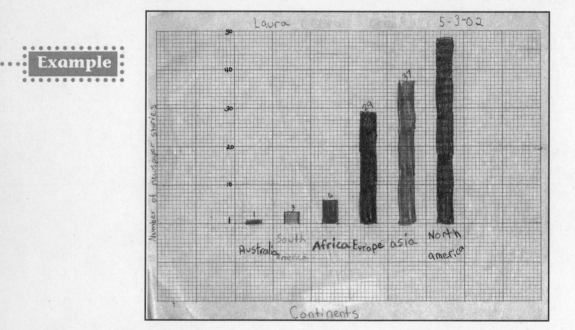

Alternative Activities

• Using a blank continent map, have students draw in the countries or cities that the news has occurred in. Then, they can graph the number of times the countries or cities have appeared in the news.

• Have students look for the important leaders of various nations, and graph how many times in a week they are in the news.

What's My Definition?

Looking for a new way to introduce social studies vocabulary to your students? This activity is sure to catch their attention. They will be so involved with the activity, they won't even realize that they are learning. In this lesson, students are presented with two definitions for a word—one correct and one incorrect. They vote on which definition they think is correct. You'll find that guessing correctly boosts their confidence.

Materials

- 8 $\frac{1}{2}$ " x 11" loose-leaf notebook paper
- Pencil

1. Prior to this activity, you will need to write down the definitions for the words you want students to learn. Then write an incorrect definition for each word as well.

2. Write the vocabulary word on the chalkboard and have the students write the word in their notebook.

3. Next, write both definitions on the board and tell the class to think about which definition would be the correct one. Then, have them vote by raising their hands for either definition number one or definition number two.

4. Erase the incorrect answer from the board and have students record the correct definition in their notes.

Examples

Barter
Definition #1—to trade an item with someone
Definition #2—to argue back and forth with someone

Ratify
Definition #1—to approve
Definition #2—to change

Alternative Activities

- Assign pairs of students different vocabulary words. Have them find the correct definition and create an incorrect definition. Then, ask them to present the vocabulary lesson to the class.

- Group students into pairs. Give each pair a vocabulary word and its definition. Ask students to create and perform a short skit that explains the word's meaning.

Who Am I?

For this activity, students have the opportunity to play a form of 20 Questions to figure out the identity of a historical figure.

1. Choose a character from the social studies unit students have recently completed. The person does not have to be a famous character. He or she could be, for example, a scribe, a New England colonist, or a Roman guard.

2. Assign one student to be the expert on that character and four students to be contestants. You may wish to review some details about this person with the "expert" student ahead of time.

3. Explain to the four contestants that they should direct questions to the historical figures that can be answered with only *yes* or *no*. They aren't allowed to just start guessing names. Explain to the historical expert that she should answer the questions to the best of her ability. She may look to you for a nod of the head if she gets stumped.

4. Tell the contestants that if they think they know who the character is, they may guess after they've asked their question.

5. After 20 questions, if none of the contestants has correctly guessed who the figure is, open it up to the rest of the class to guess.

> **Materials**
> — 8 $\frac{1}{2}$" x 11" loose-leaf notebook paper
> — Pencil
> — Resource books

Example

1. *Are you a male?* Yes
2. *Did you fight in the Revolutionary War?* Yes
3. *Were you on the American side?* Yes
4. *Did you capture any British forts?* Yes
5. *Were you from another country?* Yes
6. *Were you a general?* No

Answer: Marquis de Lafayette

Alternative Activities

• Rather than representing a historical character, the expert could choose a place or an event.

• Or, to review for a test, divide students into groups. You can play the part of the expert and each group may ask up to six questions that can be answered with *yes* or *no*. If the first group cannot correctly guess the identity of the expert after six questions, then another group gets to ask six questions and make a guess.

Who Said . . .?

We often recognize a person's career or role in society by the things she or he says. A good example of this is the following quote:

No one is prevented from being of service to the city-state.
—Pericles, an ancient Greek politician

In this activity, students use the knowledge they have gained in their study of a specific culture or time in history. Their understanding of roles in society at that time helps them write quotes that might have been said by people.

Materials
- 3-D Pattern sheets
- Colored pencils
- Tape

1. Brainstorm a list of roles people might have had in their culture. These might include scribes, priests, teachers, politicians, and farmers.

2. Give each student a copy of one of the three-dimensional shape patterns.

3. Direct students to select the same number of roles from that culture as there are sides on the three-dimensional shape.

4. Have students write a different role on each side of the three-dimensional shape.

5. Direct students to create three quotes that a person with this job might say. For example, an Egyptian scribe might say, "I have just finished with that papyrus."

6. Cut out the shape and have students assemble it by folding on the dotted lines and taping the tabs to the inside of the shape.

Example

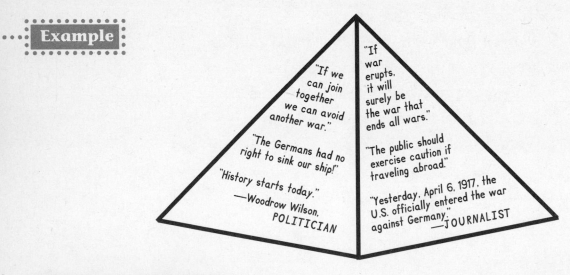

Alternative Activities

Try this activity using these topics:
- Branches of Government
- Leaders of Government
- Pioneers

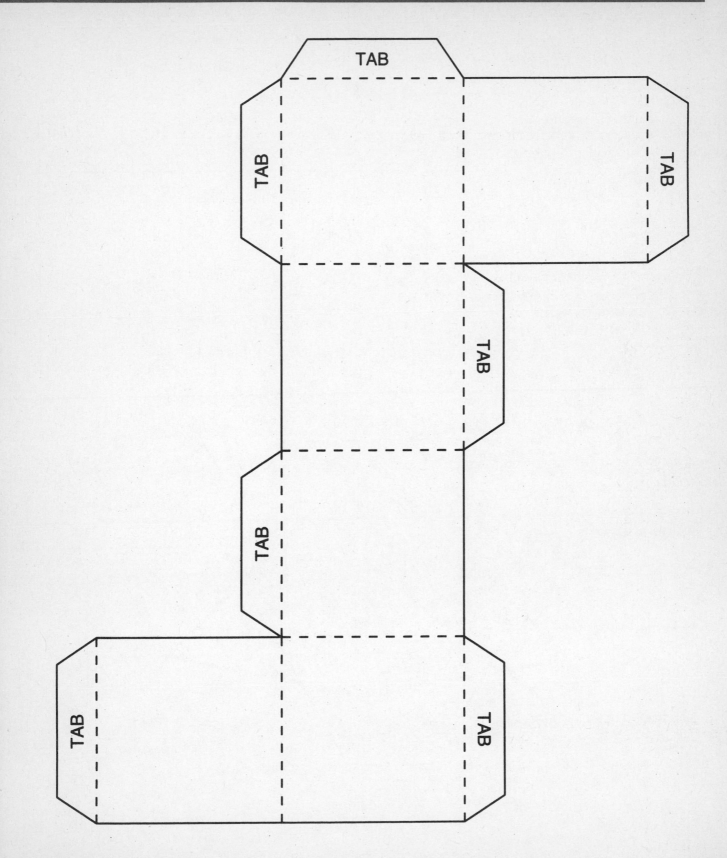

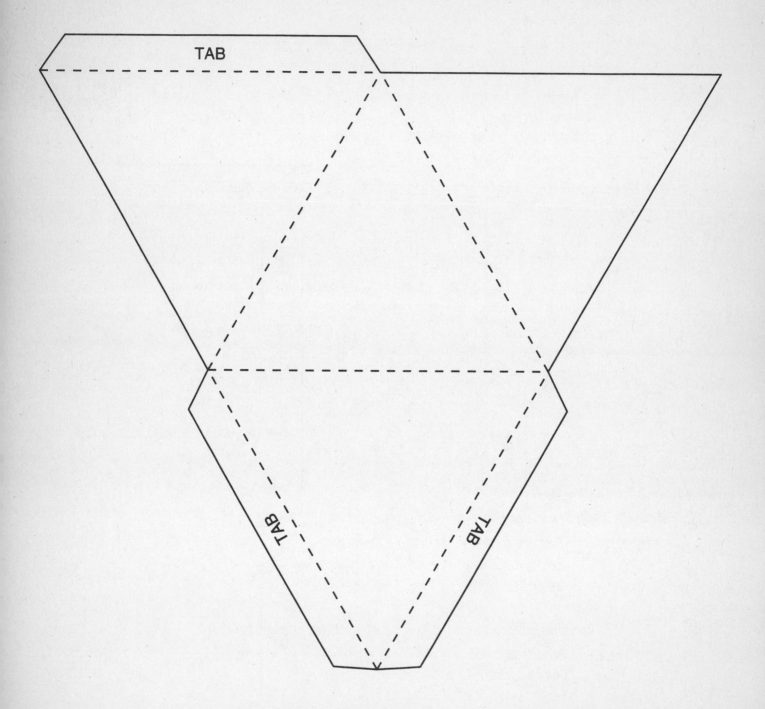

TAB

TAB

TAB

Who's Telling the Truth?

This activity is a spin-off of a classic TV game show.

1. Direct students to research a particular person from history.

2. Have them write several questions and answers about the figure. Collect the questions and answers.

3. Choose at least one question from each student, and type up a list of questions, as well as a second list with the questions and correct answers.

4. Next, type up two more lists with the questions and *incorrect* answers. The three lists with the answers will be the scripts for the contestants in the game. Make sure that you number each of the questions and that the questions in all three scripts are identical.

5. Choose three students to portray the same historical figure, and give each one a copy of the script. Only one of the students will have the script with the correct answers.

6. Cut into individual strips the questions-only sheet and pass out one question each to the remaining students. These will be the questions that the class members can ask.

7. Taking turns, in numerical order of the questions, the students will ask two of the students their question.

8. The two students who are asked the questions should respond according to the answers on their script.

9. Encourage the audience to take notes about which contestant gave correct answers and which gave incorrect answers.

10. At the end of the questioning period, have all students in the audience vote on who they think is the real historical figure.

Materials

—Question and answer sheets rewritten by teacher

Example

Ben Franklin

1. What was the name of your almanac?

      Ben Franklin #1: "Franklin's Almanac"

      Ben Franklin #2: "Poor Richard's Almanack"

      Ben Franklin #3: "Words From the Wise"

2. For which trade were you an apprentice under your brother?

      Ben Franklin #1: "I was learning to be a silversmith"

      Ben Franklin #2: "The printing trade"

      Ben Franklin #3: "Candle making"

Ben Franklin #2 has the correct answers each time.

Windows on Geography

This is a fun activity that can be created by the students or the teacher and used as a review or game.

1. Copy a state or nation map onto card stock or heavyweight paper for each child or have them neatly draw maps. This activity works best if the maps are enlarged to 8- by 10- inches or larger.

2. Have students create a series of questions about the state or country.

3. On the card-stock map, have students draw several windows using the window pattern similar to the one at right.

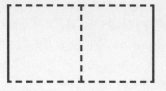

4. Then, direct them to write their questions neatly on the windows and color their maps. If using paper instead of card stock for the map, have students place a small piece of tape behind each window to keep them from tearing when they are cut.

5. Next, tell them to cut along the dotted lines on the windows.

6. Have students glue their maps (along the edges only) onto a 9- by 12-inch sheet of construction paper.

7. Direct them to open the windows and write the answers to the questions. (They can also draw a picture for the answer.)

8. Finally, have students share their window maps with the class.

Materials

- 8" x 10" map (or larger) on cardstock
- 9" x 12" constuction paper
- Window pattern
- Scissors
- Colored pencils

Example

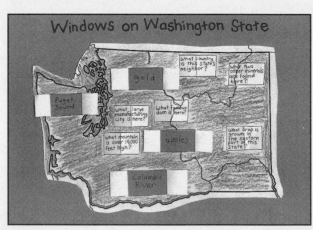

Alternative Activities

- Make a pattern that represents a specific historical time, thing, or place, such as the pyramids, a Civil War ship, the Empire State building, or an individual nation or state.
- Place trivial information in the windows and have students try to name the state it refers to.

You've Gotta Read This

With this activity, students choose an event in history and rename it as if it were a book title. Then they have the opportunity to be a book critic and write a review of the historical event.

Materials
- 8 ½" x 11" loose-leaf notebook paper
- Pencil

1. Direct students to choose an event from the social studies material recently studied.

2. Tell them to give the event a title as if it were a book.

3. Direct students to write a three-paragraph book review. The first paragraph should include three to four sentences that reveal the book's title and author, and the student's opinion of the book. In the second paragraph, the student should write a brief summary of the story (event). The last paragraph should be three or four sentences that tell to whom the students would recommend the book.

4. You can share the following example with students if you wish.

Example

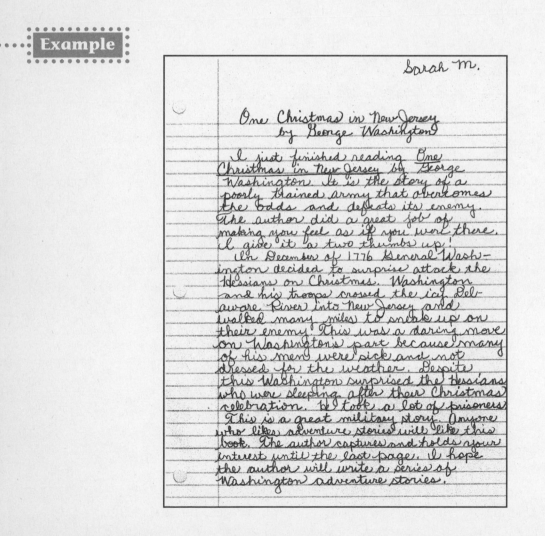

Sarah M.

One Christmas in New Jersey
by George Washington

I just finished reading One Christmas in New Jersey by George Washington. It is the story of a poorly trained army that overcomes the odds and defeats its enemy. The author did a great job of making you feel as if you were there. I give it a two thumbs up!

In December of 1776 General Washington decided to surprise attack the Hessians on Christmas. Washington and his troops crossed the icy Delaware River into New Jersey and walked many miles to sneak up on their enemy. This was a daring move on Washington's part because many of his men were sick and not dressed for the weather. Despite this Washington surprised the Hessians who were sleeping after their Christmas celebration. He took a lot of prisoners.

This is a great military story. Anyone who likes adventure stories will like this book. The author captures and holds your interest until the last page. I hope the author will write a series of Washington adventure stories.

Your Question Is . . .

Usually students are given a question and asked to find one or more answers for it. For this activity they do just the opposite. This review game is sure to stir up a little competition as well as enthusiasm.

1. Give students a name, event, date, or vocabulary word.

2. Ask them to write three social studies questions that could be answered with that name, date, event, or vocabulary word.

3. Next, have each student share one question. If someone else in the class has written that same question, then no points are scored. If the question is unique, the student scores one point. The student who has the most points at the end is the winner of that round.

4. Continue this activity as long as you wish. The final winner is the one who has scored the most points during the entire game.

Materials

- 8 $\frac{1}{2}$" x 11" loose-leaf notebook paper
- Pencil

Example

Ask students:

If the answer is "Louisiana Purchase," what is your question?

Sample Questions

- What is the name of the land Napoleon Bonaparte sold to Thomas Jefferson?

- What area were Lewis and Clark hired to explore?

- What U.S. land had the following borders: west of the Mississippi River, east of the Rocky Mountains, north of New Orleans, and south of Canada?

Name: _____

Date: _____

U.S. Outline Map

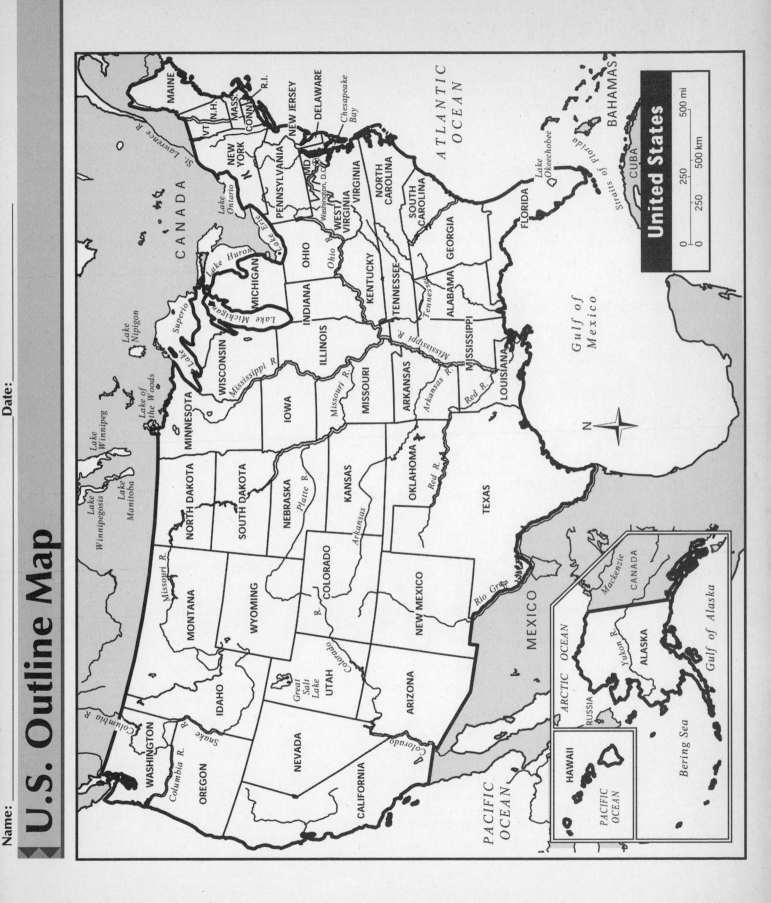

SOCIAL STUDIES ACTIVITIES KIDS CAN'T RESIST! Scholastic Professional Books

Skills Index

Analysis
Fact and Opinion Switch
Fortunately/Unfortunately
Graffiti Wall
Mirror, Mirror
Regional Trees
Then and Now
Top Ten Reasons
True/False
Who Am I?
Who's Telling the Truth?

Application
Career Moves
Culture Catalog
Flying High
Historical Diaries
Hourglass Biography Dolls
Letters From the Past
Mirror, Mirror
News and Views
Shaped Time Line
Souvenir Shopping
A Ticket to Ride
Who Said . . . ?
You've Gotta Read This!

Cause and Effect
Changing History
Fortunately/Unfortunately

Comprehension
And the Answer Is . . .
Career Moves
Have You Heard?
    News Show
Top Hits Countdown
True/False
You've Gotta Read This!

Critical Thinking
Career Moves
Fortunately/Unfortunately
Graffiti Wall
Your Question Is . . .

Drawing Conclusions
Dictionary Fun
There Must Be a Better Way
Who Am I?
Who Said . . . ?

Evaluation
Changing History
Character Fact and Opinion
Fortunately/Unfortunately
In My Defense
There Must Be a Better Way
Top Ten Reasons
Who's Telling the Truth?

Fact and Opinion
Character Fact and Opinion
Fact and Opinion Switch
Have You Heard?
    News Show

Geography
Puzzle Geography
Rebus Stories

Graphing
Buddy Maps
What's Happening?

Inferences
Dictionary Fun
Historical Diaries
Rebus Stories

Interpreting Information
Then and Now
Top Ten Reasons

Main Idea
ABC Stories
News and Views
Web Pages

Map Skills
Buddy Maps
"I Won!"
Menu Trivia
Puzzle Geography
Souvenir Shopping
A Ticket to Ride
What's Happening?

Math
"I Won!"

Multicultural Studies
Culture Catalog
"I Won!"
Menu Trivia
A Ticket to Ride

Point of View
In My Defense

Prediction
Changing History

Prior Knowledge
ABC Stories
And the Answer Is . . .
Historical Diaries
Historical Theme Park
There Must Be a Better Way
What's My Definition?

Reading for Information
Trivia Scavenger Hunt

Referencing
Dictionary Fun
Hourglass Biography Dolls
Letters From the Past
Puzzle Geography
Shaped Time Line
Trivia Scavenger Hunt
Web Pages
Who's Telling the Truth?
Windows on Geography

Sequencing
ABC Stories
Shaped Time Line

Skimming
Trivia Scavenger Hunt

Synthesis
ABC Stories
Culture Catalog
Flying High
Have You Heard?
    News Show
Historical Theme Park
Hourglass Biography Dolls
News and Views
Rebus Stories
Regional Trees
Souvenir Shopping
Top Hits Countdown
Web Pages
You've Gotta Read This!
Your Question Is . . .

Vocabulary
And the Answer Is . . .
What's My Definition?